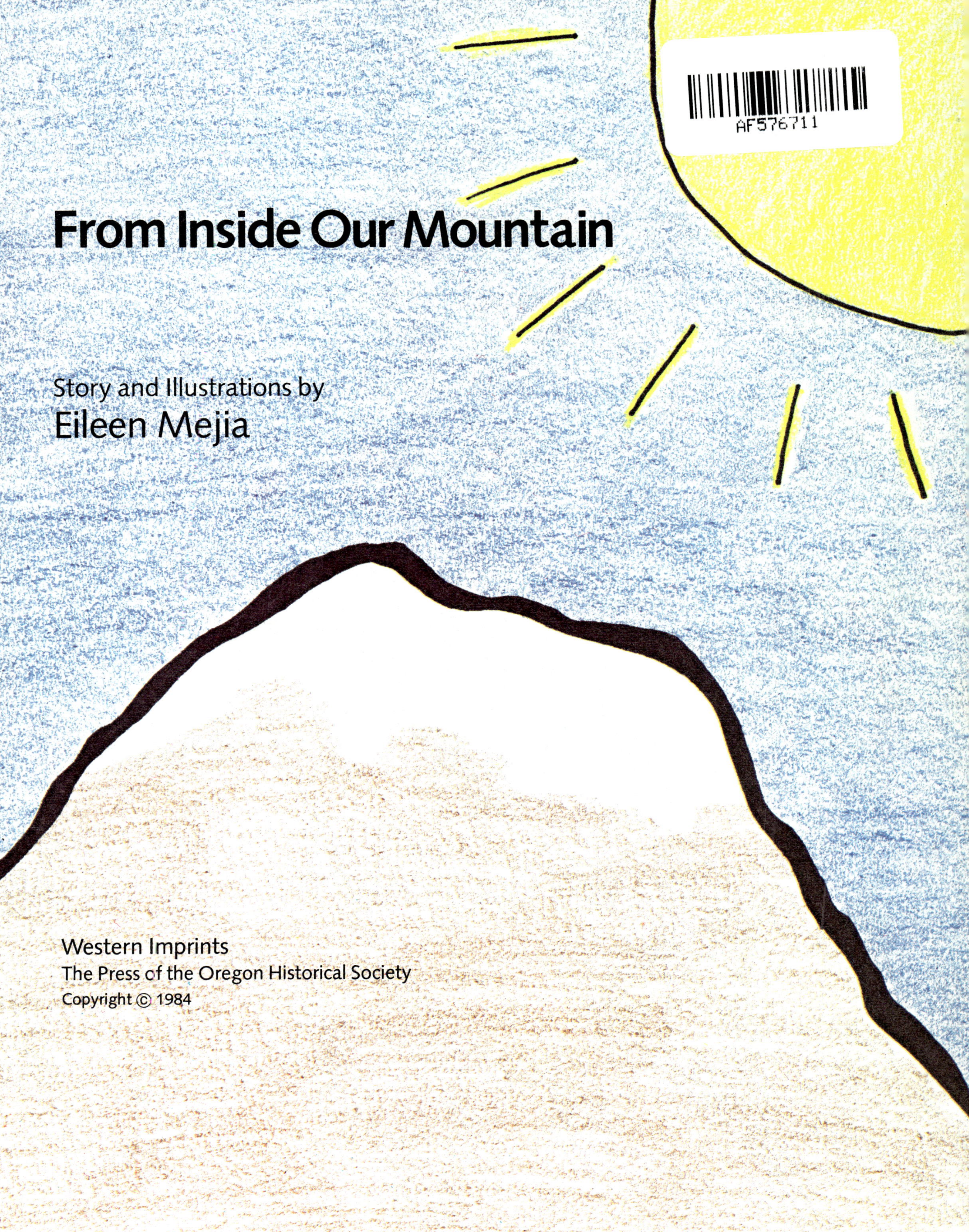
From Inside Our Mountain
Story and Illustrations by
Eileen Mejia
Western Imprints
The Press of the Oregon Historical Society
Copyright © 1984
AF576711

As long as I could remember I had lived deep inside a warm and cozy mountain. I used to be a small, gray rock then. My life was very peaceful inside my mountain. I had lots of rocky friends who sat around with me telling stories in the dark.

No one ever bothered us. Sometimes we heard the voices of people and footsteps climbing outside our walls and ceiling. Often we heard wind talk to trees who lived outside. If we listened very carefully we could hear the "scratch-scratch" of little animals digging on the surface.

One of my best friends was a shiny black rock. He always longed for excitement and change. I often listened to him wonder what it would be like to melt and flow upwards as some of our friends had done a long time ago. They had never returned to tell us what it had been like.

I didn't know I would soon find that out for myself.

One day my shiny friend and I were talking quietly when we noticed the air become warmer. The earth shook and we were jolted from our places.

After a few minutes of shaking everything became still and quiet again. My shiny friend said that it wouldn't be long before we would be able to feel for ourselves those exciting changes.

The air continued to grow warmer. We were jolted again and again. We felt softer and lighter. Now we talked excitedly about what it would be like to melt and rise.

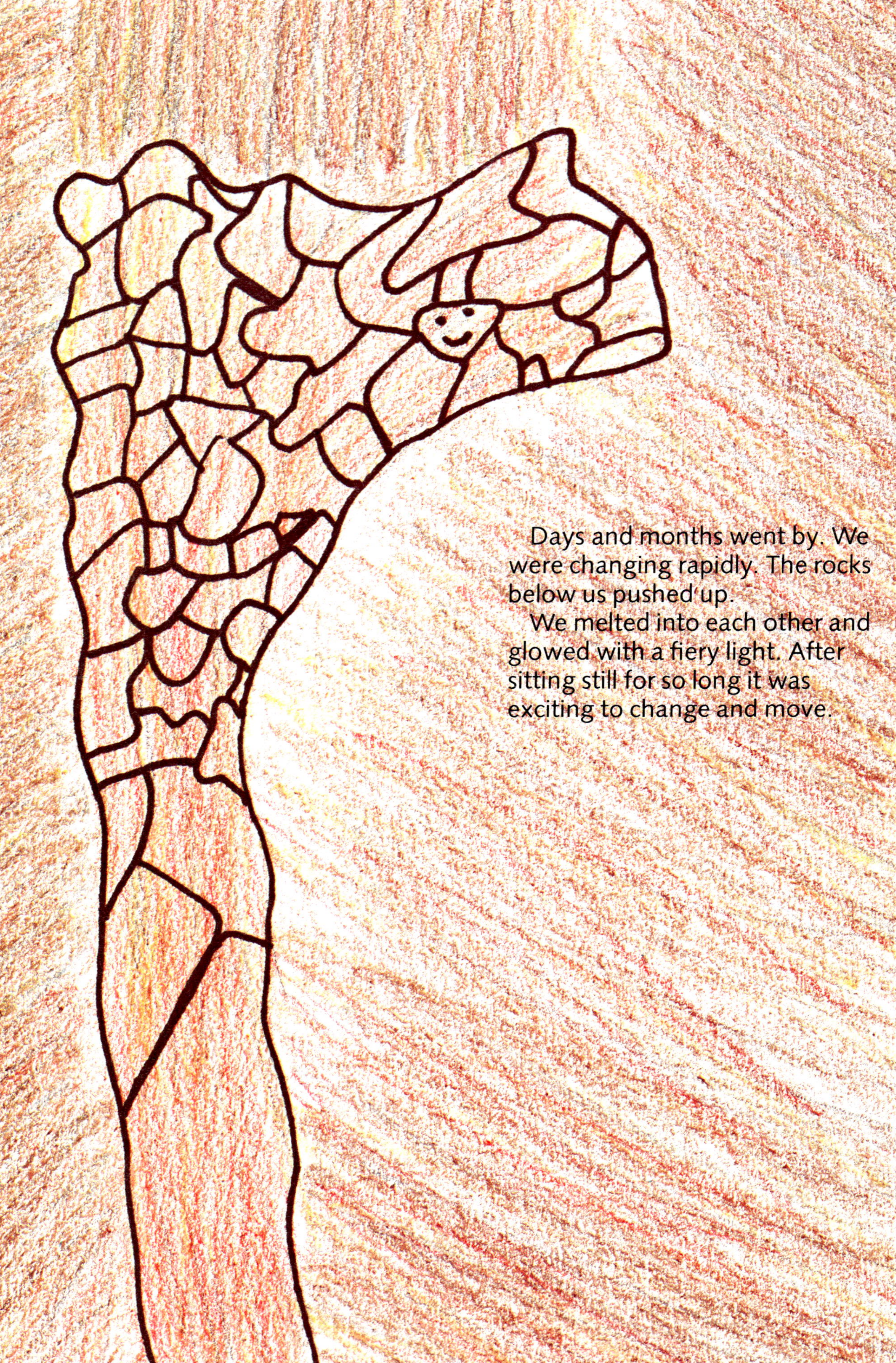

Days and months went by. We were changing rapidly. The rocks below us pushed up.

We melted into each other and glowed with a fiery light. After sitting still for so long it was exciting to change and move.

As we rose upward we flowed past rocks and clumps of dirt which had not melted.

"You will reach the outside world!" one of them told us. We quivered with excitement.

"What will it be like?" my friend asked.

"It will be filled with light and noise," an old clump of dirt replied. She said she had been blown out of the mountain a long, long time ago when she was still a rock. She said she had been blown straight up into the sky for miles before she fell back inside the mountain's warm walls.

I didn't quite believe her then, but I know now she was telling the truth.

Weeks went by. Then we felt so light-headed we rose faster and faster. Some of us flowed straight up toward our mountain roof. At the same time the rest of us flowed to one side, piled against one wall and pushed it slowly but steadily out.

My shiny friend went with the first flow, the one going toward the roof. While I helped to push out the wall, he was hurled upward faster and faster until his flow pushed a hole through the roof and rushed up into the air.

Instantly we felt cooler. We slowed down.

After a few noisy hours my shiny friend fell back down into our mountain. He was no longer a shiny rock. He was now a handful of fine, gritty ash.

"It was beautiful!" he exclaimed. "When we hit the air we exploded and shot out of the mountain. We had become millions of tiny particles. It was strange to feel so light. It took me a long time to float back down."

We sat talking and cooling down. Then several more times we heated up and pushed on the wall.

We heard helicopters in the sky. They came often now, waiting and watching our mountain.

Some of my friends exploded out the roof again and again. I wondered if I would ever see the world. I wondered if I would ever explode into fine gray ash.

That was when we all felt the great jolt. I could hear snow rumbling down the side of my wall and great loud cracking noises of trees torn away by the avalanche of snow. We heated up hotter and pressed out harder. We bubbled, splattered . . .

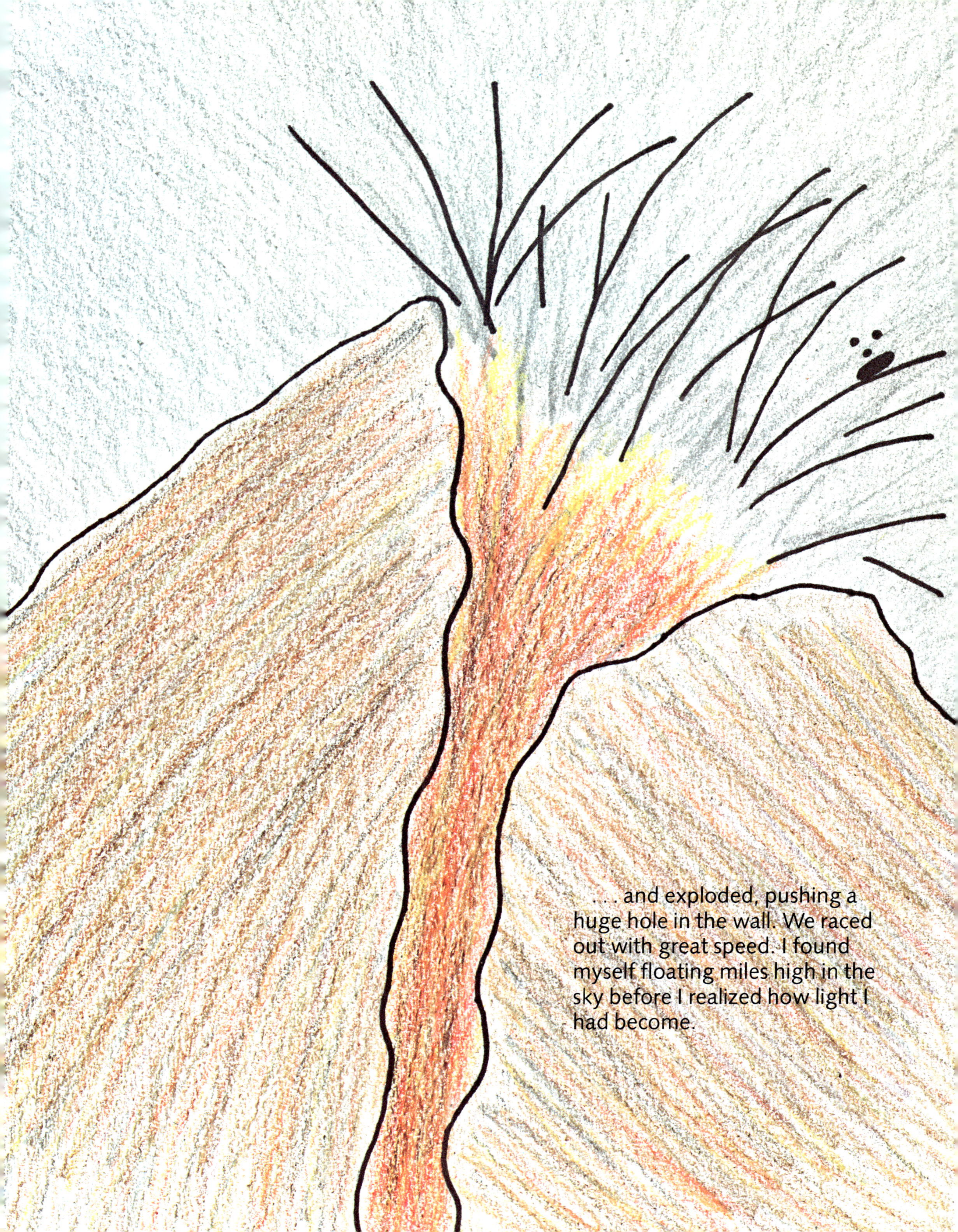

. . . . and exploded, pushing a huge hole in the wall. We raced out with great speed. I found myself floating miles high in the sky before I realized how light I had become.

A cool wind caught me. Everything was quite dark. All of my friends were with me as we floated, a large cloud of dark ash, across the outside world.

Gradually, as some of my heavier friends fell to the ground below, I saw the world become brighter. Then I, too, fell lightly toward earth. I landed softly on a blanket of ash.

After a time we had all fallen or been carried away by the wind.

The sky cleared. It was bright and blue.

Whenever the wind came up we swirled about.

I saw people. They wore masks to protect their lungs from our fine ash particles. We had landed in the center of a small town. I heard people wondering what to do with us. I felt cold and exposed.

One day I was scooped up with my friends and dropped into a truck. When it was full it started to drive off but we began to swirl up in the wind.

Someone got a hose and watered us down. We felt so heavy and the wind couldn't blow us then. I missed our warm and cozy mountain.

After a long, wet ride the truck dumped us onto a field. I was tired of the bright glare of the sky. I huddled with my friends and shivered.

Then we felt the ground shake. I looked up and saw a big plow. It was turning the earth.

As it came closer I smelled the deep rich earth open up. It reminded me of how the inside of our mountain smelled. It came closer and closer. When it reached me the big plow dug a large hole in the ground.

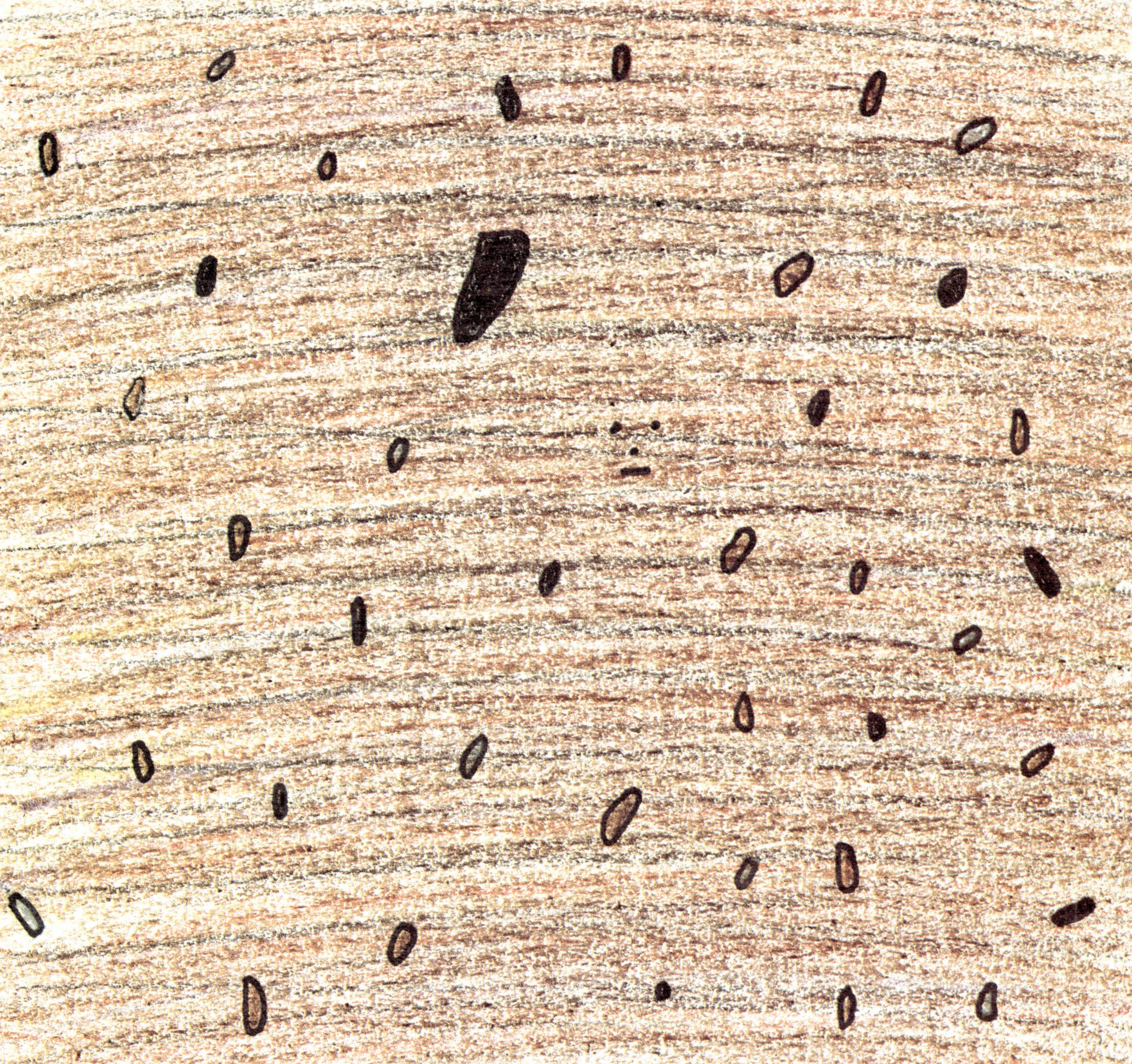

I tumbled into its cozy darkness and was covered up by a rich layer of warm, rocky dirt. I burrowed down into the earth. I sat very still and listened. It was quiet and peaceful.

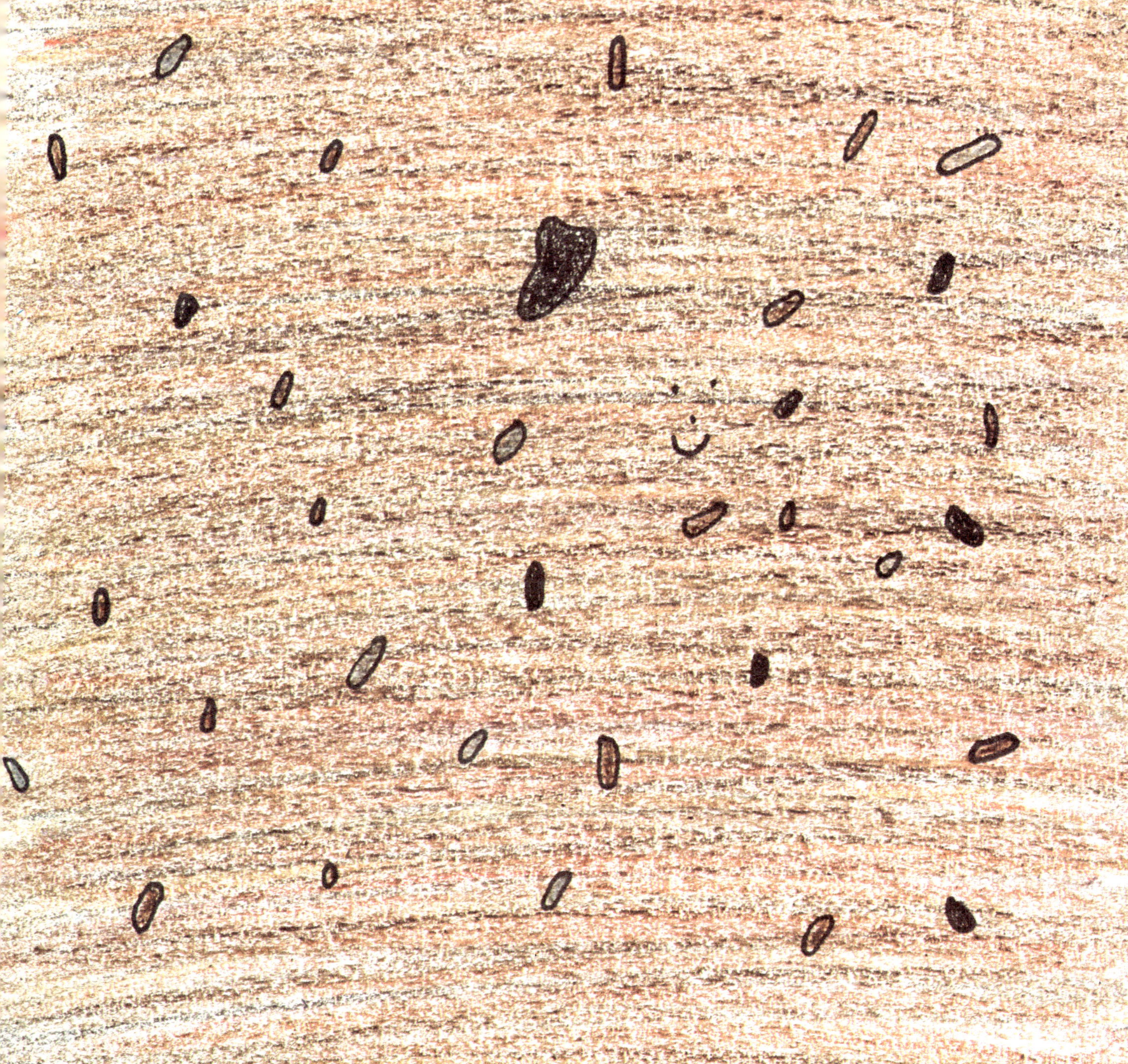

It felt good to be at rest once
again and tell stories in the dark.

Colophon

The typeface used in this book is Syntax-Antiqua, a sans serif created by the Swiss designer and professor Hans Ed. Meyer and produced by the German typefounding firm of D. Stempel AG.

This typeface design is a sans serif derived from the serif typefaces specifically designed for printing known as Garaldes, but long referred to as Old Style faces. The Garaldes still reflect the variation in thickness of pen strokes, which results in a vital, energetic modern typeface.

The typesetting for *From Inside Our Mountain* was provided by Irish Setter; Carpenter/Offutt Paper supplied the 100# Maker's Matte and 88# Legendary Duplex cover stock, color separations were produced by ColourScan; the printing and binding were accomplished by WCP Printing—all Portland firms. The illustrations were drawn by the author, Eileen Mejia, and the book was designed and produced by Western Imprints, The Press of The Oregon Historical Society.